Hogansville Public Library

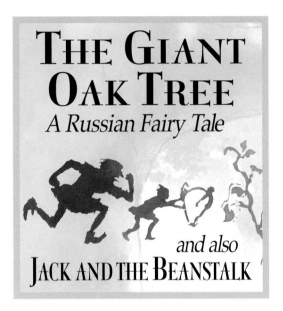

THE GIANT OAK TREE
A Russian Fairy Tale

and also
JACK AND THE BEANSTALK

by SAVIOUR PIROTTA
and ALAN MARKS

SEA-TO-SEA
Mankato Collingwood London

This edition first published in 2008 by
Sea-to-Sea Publications
1980 Lookout Drive
North Mankato
Minnesota 56003

Text copyright © Saviour Pirotta 2004, 2008
Illustrations copyright © Alan Marks 2004

Printed in China

Library of Congress Cataloging-in-Publication Data

Pirotta, Saviour.
  The giant oak tree / by Saviour Pirotta and Alan Marks.
      p. cm. -- (Once upon a world)
  Summary: Presents two tales to compare and contrast, the first one from Russia and the
second one from   England.
  ISBN 978-1-59771-080-0
  1. Fairy tales. [1. Fairy tales. 2. Folklore.] I. Marks, Alan, 1957- II. Title.

PZ8.P6672Gi 2007
[398.2]--dc22
                                                        2007060716

9 8 7 6 5 4 3 2

Published by arrangement with the Watts Publishing Group Ltd, London.

Editor: Rachel Cooke
Series design: Jonathan Hair

Contents

Once upon a time

Have you ever tricked someone into letting you have something you wanted? Or been tempted to do so? Many old myths and folk tales across the world are about characters called tricksters who delight in causing mischief.

Tricksters often take the form of an animal but have the intelligence and cunning of a human. Native Americans tell stories of Raven, who has to trick the gods in order to give light to mankind, while in Africa and the Caribbean, tales of Ananse, the spider, are very popular. In *The Giant Oak Tree*, a Russian story retold here, the hero of the story is a clever rooster.

The tricksters are not just clever deceivers, they are also usually the underdog—achieving a happy ending against the odds.

In *The Giant Oak Tree*, the
rooster—and the old couple
he helps—win out against the
wealth and power of a knight.
The same is true of "giant-
killers," such as Jack in the story
retold at the end of this book. Jack is
something of a fool but, like other tricksters—in
this case a human one—he still outwits the ogre.

Like all good fairytales, trickster stories have a
good sprinkling of magic in them. Jack's luck
changes when he plants some magic beans while
in *The Giant Oak Tree*, the old couple, Masha and
Marik, make their fortune through an acorn. Both
these magical seeds lead to adventures in fabulous
lands above the clouds.

It is perhaps the mixture of magic and winning
against the odds that makes trickster stories
so popular. People over the centuries
have been able to see themselves in
the trickster heroes—and hope that
they, too, may one day find a hen
that will lay golden eggs for them.

The Giant Oak Tree

Once there was an old couple called Marik and Masha. They lived in a tumbledown cottage on the edge of a great forest where, it was said, witches and wizards roamed at night. Behind the cottage was a stream and beyond the stream a little field where Marik and Masha grew turnips and beets, which they boiled up for stew. It was the only food they had tasted for years.

One fall it got so cold the beets froze and rotted underground, and starving rats gnawed the turnips, leaving only the stalks to perish in the frost.

"The holy saints have pity on us," cried Masha, "we have nothing to eat at all."

"The saints will not let us die," Marik consoled her. "We'll go into the woods and find some food."

Their stomachs rumbling with hunger, the couple put on their threadbare coats and trudged across the frozen stream into the forest. All day long they searched for something to eat but in vain: not a single nut or berry was to be had. Masha was sure they were going to starve when, quite by chance, they came across a clearing. In the middle of it was an ancient oak tree and strewn all over the ground were hundreds upon hundreds of ripe acorns, gleaming in the dusk like pearls.

"It's a miracle," gasped Masha. "We're saved." And she fell to the ground and stuffed handful after handful of acorns into her mouth.

When the pair had eaten their fill, they filled a sack and dragged it home. There they heaved the sack onto the table and gorged themselves again, relishing the bitter fruit as if it were roast goose with apple

sauce, or fried sausages with sweet onions.

  When they were full to bursting, Marik
swept all the remaining acorns
back in the sack—all
except for one tiny one,
which fell unnoticed
through a hole in the
floorboards and landed
in the cellar below.

"Marik, there's someone knocking at the door," said Masha a week or so later.

"There's no one there, dear," muttered her husband, looking outside just to make sure.

"But I can hear knocking," insisted Masha.

Marik pricked up his ears. Yes, he could hear knocking too. Under his feet! Was there a burglar in the cellar? A wild boar? A witch? Fetching a lamp, he opened the creaking cellar door to investigate.

"It's a tree," he called back to Masha. "It's grown all over the cellar. The branches are scraping against the kitchen floor."

"Chop it down," replied his wife. "We need more firewood."

"It's an oak," said Marik. "Let's keep it. In time we will have our own supply of acorns."

That very same day he removed the kitchen floor, stacking the worn floorboards outside on the woodpile. Strengthened by the light, the sapling spread its branches, growing faster and thicker until it had filled every corner of the little cottage. Soon its topmost twigs were searching out the cracks in the ceiling, eager to find a way out.

Marik, fearing the house would collapse on him and Masha, pulled it down. He used the wood from the old building to build a cosy treehouse. It had a front door they could reach with a ladder, and a window looking south to where the swallows would be returning in the spring.

Not long afterward, the sack of life-saving
acorns ran out. There was no chance of
finding any more now that the ground lay
under a sheet of ice as thick as a coffin lid.
Marik said: "Let me climb up the oak. I
might find some eggs in a nest."

"Bring lots," said Masha, "then we
could eat some and paint the rest
to hang on the branches for
good luck."

Marik put on his
coat and started
climbing up the tree, using
the branches like the rungs on
a ladder.

"The saints be praised," he said to
himself, "this tree must be growing
through the gates of heaven itself."

Not quite. The tree stopped just above the clouds and Marik came to a field, floating there in the sky, embroidered with flowers and smelling like spring. He planted his foot on it and it didn't give way. So he walked across the field through the nodding flowers till he came to a castle.

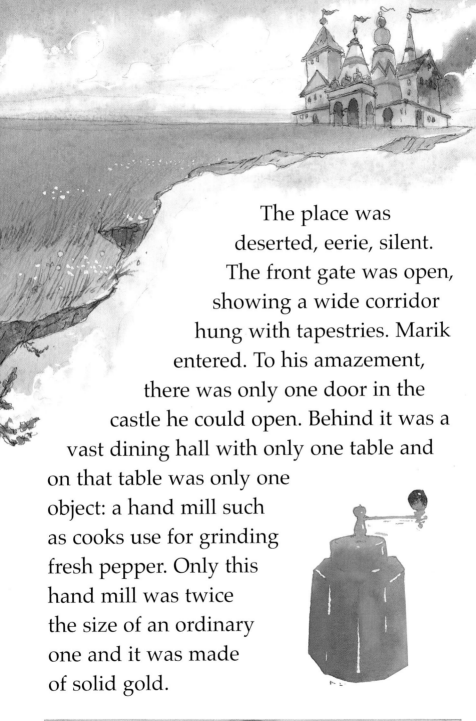

The place was
deserted, eerie, silent.
The front gate was open,
showing a wide corridor
hung with tapestries. Marik
entered. To his amazement,
there was only one door in the
castle he could open. Behind it was a
vast dining hall with only one table and
on that table was only one
object: a hand mill such
as cooks use for grinding
fresh pepper. Only this
hand mill was twice
the size of an ordinary
one and it was made
of solid gold.

Marik was wondering where to go next
when a rooster flew in through the only
window and landed on his shoulder,
shaking a coxcomb as red as fire.

"Take the hand mill, it's yours," cried the
rooster.

"Mine? How could it be mine?" asked
Marik. "I've never seen this thing before."
He was not at all surprised to hear the
rooster talk. After all, had he not
just climbed a giant oak and
discovered a new land in
the sky?

"It is mine to give,"
said the rooster. "Take
it, and take me with
you, too. I cannot
bear to greet
another sunrise in
this deserted
castle."

So Marik put the hand mill carefully under one arm and, with the rooster clinging to his shoulder, climbed down the oak to the treehouse.

"A nice plump bird for the pot,"
exclaimed Masha when she saw the rooster.
The bird, settling on a branch out of her
reach, cackled loudly and said,
"You do not need to twist my
neck for your supper, good
madam. Just turn the
handle on the mill and see
what happens."
Masha took the hand mill
and gave the handle a turn.

To her amazement, a pancake fell out,
warm and fragrant with toasted sugar. She
pinched a little in her fingers and popped it
in her mouth. Mmm, what buttery softness!
What sugary sweetness! Masha started to
drool. She turned the handle again. Another
pancake followed, this one smothered with
fresh cream. Soon the table was piled high
with pancakes, one for every turn of the mill.
Masha and Marik fell upon them and, with
no regard for manners, devoured them all!

Then the rooster cried, "So much for the appetizers. Now turn the handle the other way and see what happens next."

Masha did as the bird instructed and, this time, out of the mill tumbled a pie. An apple and cherry pie! And what a pie! It smelled delicious and tasted divine. Marik and Masha wolfed it down. Then they cranked out another…a dozen more…a larder full.

When they couldn't eat any more, they crumbled the crusts and fed the rooster, the birds on the windowsill, and the foxes that had been lured to the tree by the aroma of baking pastry. At last, their stomachs stretched to bursting, Masha and Marik fell into bed.

"Ahoy there, anyone home?" Marik looked out of the window. A nobleman was coming down the forest path on his white charger. He seemed lost and tired; his fine clothes were soaked through with rain.

He'd been out hunting with his friends, the knight explained, but he'd become separated from his party. Could he come into the treehouse and shelter from the rain?

"You can have a pancake and a pie, too, while you're waiting for the sky to clear," laughed Masha, welcoming the fine lord up the ladder. She was eager to share her good fortune with others.

The knight's eyes grew as wide as dinner plates when he saw the hand mill cranking out food.

"How much do you want for that marvel?" he asked. "I'm willing to pay anything. A treasure chest full of gold or diamonds. A corner of my estate, even."

"What would old people like us do with land and diamonds?" said Masha, putting the hand mill back in the larder. "This is treasure enough for us."

But the noble lord had never taken no for an answer in all his life. Such a useful bauble, he thought, such magic. He had to have it. Imagine his friends' faces when he set the mill to work at dinner.

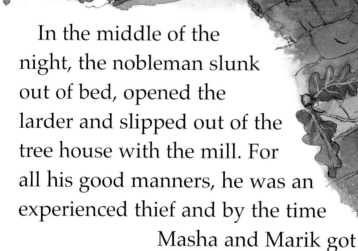

In the middle of the
night, the nobleman slunk
out of bed, opened the
larder and slipped out of the
tree house with the mill. For
all his good manners, he was an
experienced thief and by the time
Masha and Marik got
up, he was already out
of the forest.

"We've been robbed,"
howled Masha.

"Swindled," cried Marik.

"I'll show him!"
Masha reached for
her iron ladle.

"No, I'll chase the thief," said the rooster.
"I am quicker on my wings than you on
your aged feet."

And off he flew, diving and dodging
through the trees, because roosters,
especially plump ones, cannot fly very high.

When he caught up with the nobleman,
the thief was galloping up the drive to his
castle. The rooster perched on the front gate
and crowed, a little out of breath:

"Cock-a-doodle-do,
Cock-a-doodle-do,
Give me back the hand mill, you."

The knight, getting off his horse, turned angrily to his guards. "Catch that bird and drown it in the well."

The guards, all swords and spears, chased the rooster all around the estate. When they caught him, they threw him down the well.

The rooster, shaking his coxcomb with outrage, chanted:

"Open beak
Drink the water.
Every drop
Do not falter."

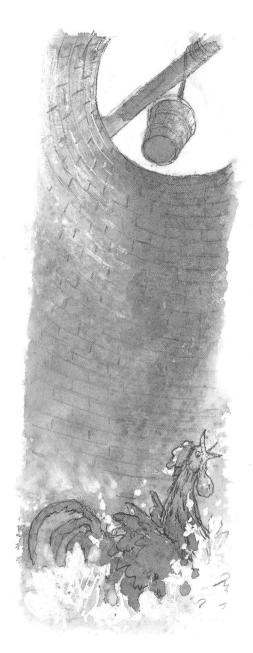

And he opened his mouth and drank all
the water in the well till not a drop was left.
Then he shook his feathers dry and flew
back to the castle keep.

By now the knight was getting
ready for bed. The rooster
perched himself on the
balcony outside his
bedroom and crowed,
quite out of breath:

"Cock-a-doodle-do,
Cock-a-doodle-do,
Give me back the hand mill, you."

"I thought I'd seen the last of that annoying chicken," snapped the knight. And he ordered his servants to roast the bird.

The servants chased the rooster with their pots and pans. When they caught him, trying to regain his breath in a rosebush, they thrust him in the oven.

The rooster was not at all put out. His red coxcomb matching the flames, he chanted:

"Open beak
Spill the water.
Every drop
Do not falter."

And all the water he had drunk in the well poured out of his beak and flooded the oven, putting out the fire and filling the kitchen with steam.

The rooster preened his feathers, straightened out his coxcomb, and stole into the knight's bedroom. He perched himself on the carved headboard and wheezed, hardly able to talk:

"Cock-a-doodle-do,
Cock-a-doodle-do,
Give me back the hand mill, you."

The nobleman's wife, who couldn't sleep on account of her husband's snoring, sat up and screamed: "There's a ghost in the room!" And she flung off the bedclothes and ran out. The knight, woken by her shrieks, followed her. Then his guards and servants—seeing their master had nothing on but his wedding ring—ran after him with a fur coat. They left the castle gates open and forgot all about the hand mill on the kitchen table.

The rooster picked up the mill in his beak and flew back home to Masha and Marik. Pausing only for a large breakfast, the old couple set about moving their house further up the tree, where no thief could reach it. And there they and the rooster feasted on pancakes and pies for the rest of their lives!

Jack and the Beanstalk

No one knows for sure when *Jack and the Beanstalk* was first told. In 1734, *The Story of Jack Spriggins and the Enchanted Bean* was published. Its comic feel suggests it was already an old favorite with British children. Joseph Jacobs wrote a version in 1890 and his story is the best known one today.

There was once a poor widow who had a son named Jack, and a cow named Milky White. One morning, she said: "Jack we'll have to sell the cow. Take it to the market, and make sure you get a good price for it."

Jack hadn't gone far when he met an old man. "I'll give you five beans for that cow," said the man.

"Be off with you," said Jack.

"But these are special beans," said the man. "Plant them overnight, and by

morning they'll have grown right up to the sky."

So Jack handed over Milky White and returned home with the beans. When his mother saw them, she got so angry she hurled them out of the window.

The next morning Jack looked out of the window—and what do you think he saw? Why, the beans had sprung up into a big beanstalk that went right up till it reached the sky.

Jack got dressed quickly and started climbing up the beanstalk. When he got to the top, he found a long broad road. He walked on till he came to a big tall house, and on the doorstep there was a big tall woman.

"Could you give me some breakfast?" asked Jack.

"It's breakfast you'll be if you don't move off," said the woman. "My man is an ogre and there's nothing he likes better than baked boys on toast."

"But I've had nothing to eat since yesterday," said Jack.

The ogre's wife took pity on him. She led Jack into the kitchen, and gave him some bread and cheese. Jack had only just started eating when—thump! thump! thump!—the whole house began to tremble.

"It's my old man," said the ogre's wife. And she bundled Jack into the oven. The giant came in, sniffed the air and roared:

"Fee-fi-fo-fum,
I smell the blood of an Englishman."

"Don't be silly," said his wife. "There are no Englishmen here. I've boiled you a cow for breakfast."

The ogre had his breakfast, and after that he went to a big chest and took some bags of gold. He sat down and counted and recounted his gold till at last he fell asleep.

When he heard the snoring, Jack crept out from the oven, took one of the bags, and pelted off to the beanstalk. Down, down, down he climbed till he got home.

His mother welcomed the gold and, for a while, they lived like kings. But the gold came to an end, and Jack decided to try his luck up the beanstalk again.

He climbed up till he came to the road and found the big tall house again. There, sure enough, was the ogre's wife standing on the doorstep.

"Could you give me something to eat?" asked Jack.

"Aren't you the youngster who came here once before?" said the big tall woman. "Do you know, that very day you came, my man missed a bag of gold?"

"I could tell you something about that," said Jack, "but I'm so hungry I can't speak."

The woman was so curious that she took him inside. He had scarcely begun eating when they heard the giant's steps, and his wife hid Jack in the oven again.

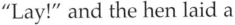

All happened as it did before. In came the ogre, roaring:

"Fee-fi-fo-fum,
I smell the blood of an Englishman."

But he sat down happily enough to eat his boiled cow.

Then the ogre fetched a hen, said to it:

"Lay!" and the hen laid a golden egg. Before long he fell asleep and the house shook with his snoring. Jack crept out of the oven, grabbed the hen, and ran with it till he got home.

Well, the hen was a prize indeed, but it wasn't long before Jack decided to try his luck once more at the ogre's house and he climbed up the beanstalk again.

This time he stole to the big tall house, crept past the big tall woman as she came out to get a pail of water, and hid in the kettle. He hadn't been there long when the ogre came in. Once again the ogre roared:

"Fee-fi-fo-fum,
I smell the blood of an Englishman."

"Stop that nonsense," scolded his wife.

The ogre ate his breakfast and afterwards fetched a golden harp. "Sing," he ordered it, and the harp sang most beautifully till the ogre fell asleep.

Then Jack crept out of the kettle, caught hold of the golden harp, and dashed with it toward the door. The harp called out, "Master! Master!" and the ogre woke up.

Jack ran as fast as he could. The ogre came rushing after him but Jack got to the beanstalk before him. Down, down, down he climbed with the ogre following. When he was nearly home Jack called out, "Mother! Bring me an axe."

His mother rushed out with the axe. Jack got hold of it and —chop, chop, chop—the beanstalk toppled over. The ogre fell with it to the ground —and to his death.

Then Jack and his mother had no more worries. They held concerts with the golden harp, sold the golden eggs— and lived happily ever after.

Taking it further

Once you've read both stories in this book, there is lots more you can think and talk about. There's plenty to write about, too.

• To begin with, think about what is the same and what is different about the two stories. Talk about this with other people. Which story do you prefer and why? Does either story remind you of any other famous fairytales?

• Can you think of an animal that would make a good trickster? Compare this with your friends' ideas and see what they think.

• Both the stories in this book are about magic lands in the sky that you get to by climbing up a tree or beanstalk. Can you think of any other way you could get to a magic land above the clouds?

• Imagine you are either Jack or the rooster from the stories. How might you change what they do to help the other characters? Would you need some magical assistance or would you just get by on your wits?